W9-BCA-054

My Silly Body

Why Do I Sneeze?

by Molly Kolpin

Consulting Editor: Gail Saunders-Smith, PhD

Consultant: Marjorie Hogan, MD
Department of Pediatrics
Hennepin County Medical Center

CAPSTONE PRESS
a capstone imprint

Pebble Plus is published by Capstone Press,
1710 Roe Crest Drive, North Mankato, Minnesota 56003
www.capstonepub.com

Library of Congress Cataloging-in-Publication Data
Kolpin, Molly, author.
Why do I sneeze? / by Molly Kolpin.
pages cm. — (Pebble plus. My silly body)
Summary: "Simple text and full-page photos describe what happens in the body that makes us sneeze"— Provided by publisher.
Audience: Ages 4–8.
Audience: K to grade 3.
Includes bibliographical references and index.
ISBN 978-1-4914-2108-6 (library binding)
ISBN 978-1-4914-2349-3 (eBook PDF)
1. Sneezing—Juvenile literature. 2. Allergy—Juvenile literature. 3. Human physiology—Juvenile literature. I. Title.
PQ121.K65 2015
612.2'3—dc23   2014022198

Editorial Credits
Michelle Hasselius, editor; Kazuko Collins, designer; Gina Kammer, media researcher; Morgan Walters, production specialist

Photo Credits
Alamy: Adams Picture Library t/a apl, 9; Dreamstime: Gunjan Karun, 13, Wavebreakmedia Ltd, 19; Glow Images: Science Faction/Superstock, 5; iStockphotos: JamieWilson, 17; Shutterstock: antpkr, 7, Catalin Petolea, cover, Digital Storm, 11, GVictoria, 21, s_oleg, 15
Design Elements: Shutterstock: Eliks (spotted design), HAKKI ARSLAN (sun beams)

Note to Parents and Teachers

The My Silly Body set supports national science standards related to life science. This book describes and illustrates why we sneeze. The images support early readers in understanding the text. The repetition of words and phrases helps early readers learn new words. This book also introduces early readers to subject-specific vocabulary words, which are defined in the Glossary section. Early readers may need assistance to read some words and to use the Table of Contents, Glossary, Read More, Internet Sites, and Index sections of the book.

Printed in the United States of America in Stevens Point, Wisconsin.
102014   008479WZS15

Table of Contents

In the Nose It Goes

Why do I sneeze?

You sneeze to blast away germs and other particles. Sneezing keeps you and your nose healthy.

A sneeze can travel up to 100 miles (161 kilometers) per hour.

Germs, dust, and pollen are common sneeze starters. These particles enter your nose through the air you breathe.

Tiny hairs inside your nose catch the particles. The hairs tickle your nose. This causes sensors to tell your brain to start a sneeze.

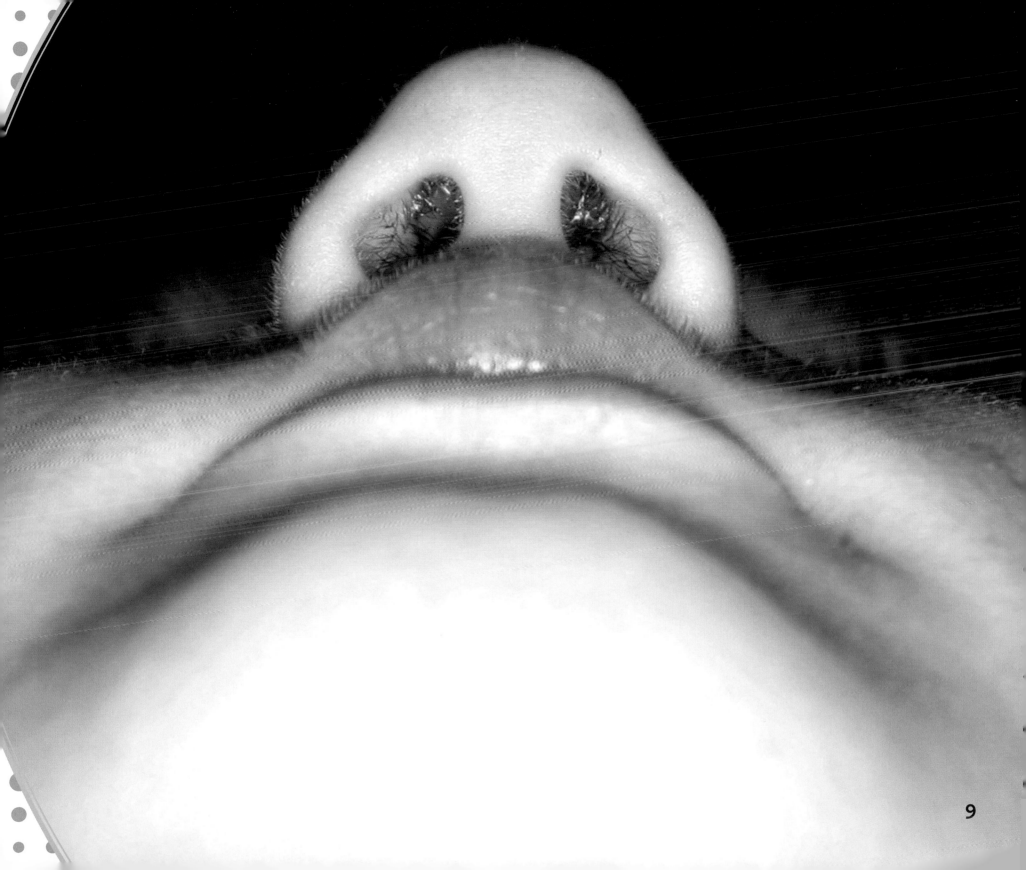

The Not-So-Simple Sneeze

You have a special area in your brain called the sneeze center. When it's time to sneeze, your sneeze center sends messages to your muscles.

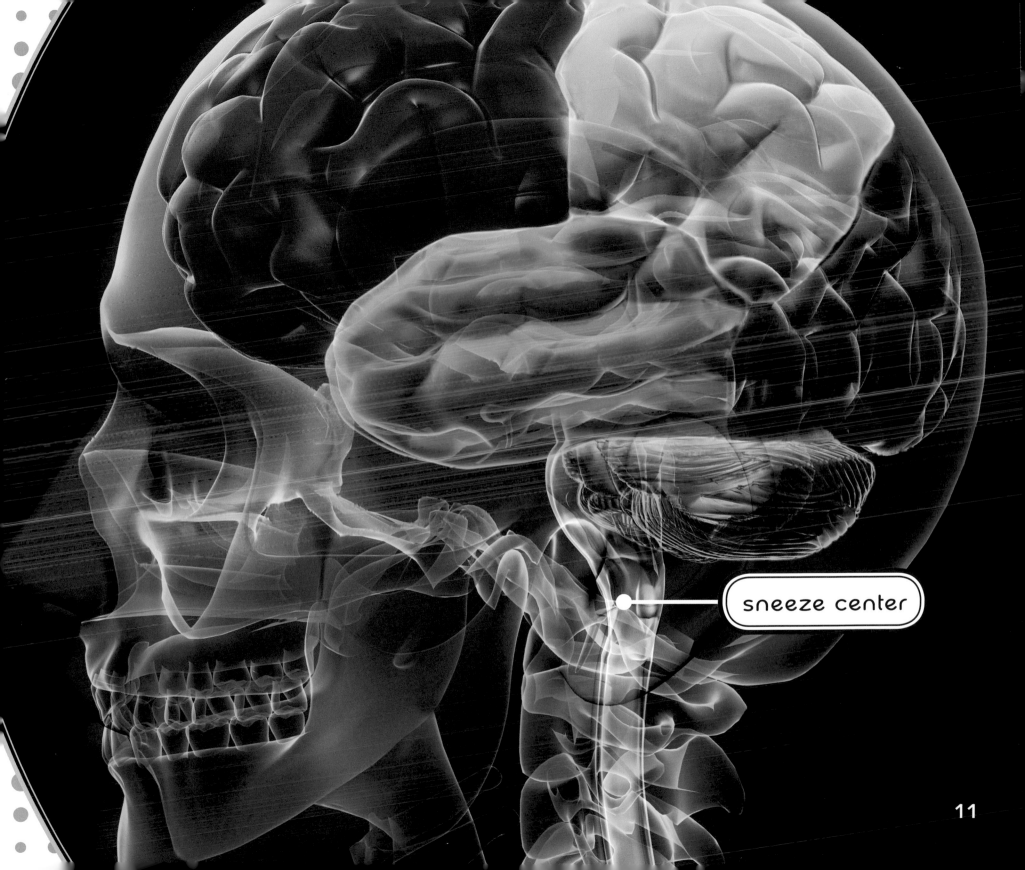

sneeze center

The muscles in your stomach, chest, throat, and eyelids help you sneeze. Thanks to them your body can get rid of what causes sneezes.

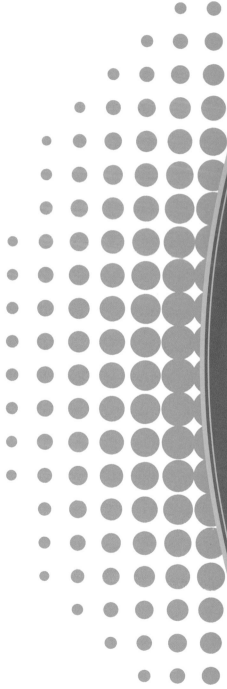

Most people shut their eyes when they sneeze.

Reasons for Sneezes

Germs and dust aren't the only reasons you sneeze. Some people sneeze after looking at bright lights.

People might also sneeze
if they have colds or allergies.
Allergies can cause people
to sneeze from things
such as mold or pet hair.

Wash your hands after you sneeze to avoid spreading germs.

Achoo!

Sometimes people pinch their noses to stop sneezes. But remember sneezes keep you healthy. It's best to let them out.

Glossary

allergy—having a reaction such as a runny nose, watery eyes, or sneezing when around or eating certain things; people may be allergic to plants, animals, dust, or certain kinds of food

crook—bend or curve

germ—a tiny living thing that can cause illnesses

muscle—a part of the body that helps you move, lift, or push

particle—a tiny piece of something

pollen—powdery grains that come from flowering plants

sensor—a body part that sends messages to the brain

Read More

Miller, Madison. *What Happens When I Sneeze?* My Body Does Strange Stuff! New York: Gareth Stevens Publishing, 2014.

Minden, Cecilia. *Keep It Clean: Achoo!* 21st Century Basic Skills Library Level 1. Ann Arbor, Mich.: Cherry Lake Pub., 2010.

Royston, Angela. *Twitches and Sneezes*. Disgusting Body Facts. Chicago: Raintree, 2010.

Internet Sites

FactHound offers a safe, fun way to find Internet sites related to this book. All of the sites on FactHound have been researched by our staff.

Here's all you do:

Visit *www.facthound.com*

Type in this code: 9781491421086

Super-cool stuff! Check out projects, games and lots more at **www.capstonekids.com**

Critical Thinking Using the Common Core

There is an area in your brain called the sneeze center. How does the sneeze center help you sneeze? Use the text to help you with your answer. (Key Ideas and Details)

Turn to page 21. What is happening in the photo? Why do you think this is a good way to sneeze? (Integration of Knowledge and Ideas)

Index

Word Count: 202
Grade: 1
Early-Intervention Level: 20